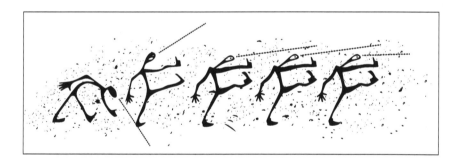

Modern Art: An Exhibition in Criticism

by Michael Curtis
Designed by Patricia Hord Graphik Design

Published by The National Civic Art Society

300 New Jersey Ave. NW
Ste. 900
Washington, DC 20001

www.civicart.org
Copyright 2022

ISBN: 979-8-9859668-0-0

MODERN ART
AN EXHIBITION IN CRITICISM

BY MICHAEL CURTIS

MODERN ART: AN EXHIBITION IN CRITICISM

TO P, B & J

ACKNOWLEDGEMENTS

Evan Mantyk, Monica Mason, Arthur Mortensen, Joseph Salemi, Justin Shubow, and Leo Yankevich for aesthetic advice and technical guidance.

Expansive Poetry Online, Mobius, Pennsylvania Review, Pivot, The Society of Classical Poets for first publishing many poems of this collection.

MODERN ART: AN EXHIBITION IN CRITICISM

MODERN ART;
YOU DON'T UNDERSTAND IT?

I DO, AND I CAN'T STAND IT.

CONTENTS

Foreward 1
Save Me, O Lord 3
Picture Gallery 4
    Casimir Malevich 5
    Piet Mondrian 6
    Gertrude Stein 7
    Constantin Brancusi 8
    Mies Van Der Rohe 9
    Walter Gropius 10
    Franz Kline 11
    William Carlos Williams 12
    Tristan Tzara 13
    David Smith 14
    Le Corbusier 15
    Hans Hoffman 16
    Alberto Giacometti 17
    Ad Reinhardt 18
    Marcel Duchamp 19
    Mark Rothko 20
    Barnett Newman 21
    Pablo Picasso 22
    Adolph Gottlieb 23
    Alexander Calder III 24
    Man Ray 25

MODERN ART: AN EXHIBITION IN CRITICISM

Joseph Alberts 26
Jean Arp 27
Giorgio De Chirico 28
Peggy Guggenheim 29
Clifford Still 30
Philip Guston 31
Andy Warhol 32
Henry Moore 33
William de Kooning 34
Salvador Dali 35
Robert Motherwell 36
Francis Bacon 37
John Cage 38
Clement Greenberg 39
Roy Lichtenstein 40
Robert Rauschenberg 41
Robert Indiana 42
Barbara Rose 43
Frank Gehry 44
Claes Oldenberg 45
Jasper Johns 46
Richard Serra 47
Cindy Sherman 48
Jeffrey Koons 49

Concert Hall 50
Whitman Proposes 51
Avant-Garde March 52
Hear! Hear! For the Sin in Sincere 53
Barbarity Renewed 54

Saint Cecilia Jones 58
Mulberry Lane 59

Lecture Series 61
Four Freedoms of Modern Art 62
Cubism Squared 63
So Ho So 64
Futurism Finish 65
A Better Jackson Pollock 66
The Course Unfired 67
Beat of The Scream 68
Poets Scratch 69
Mnemosyne 70
Strip the Poet 71
Praise Song 72
Budding Michaelangelos 73
Post Ism 74
XXth Century Modern Speaks 75
Spoken at the Dedication: Art Museum Additions, 1940-2005 76
Slow the Wit 77
So Long Words: Modern Art Monographs 79
The New Moo: Stock Modernism 80
Raison d'Être 81
Avant-Garde Lament 82
Modern Face 83
Must We 84
Extracted Ex Pressions 85
Minimalist 86
Censor Me 87
Ring Out the New 1990 88

MODERN ART: AN EXHIBITION IN CRITICISM

FOREWARD
BY DAVID TALBOT

No one familiar with Michael Curtis would call him unexacting. His work displays a keen, critical mind, bringing beauty to the senses and banishing ugliness where he finds it. *Modern Art* is a playful exercise in the latter. It is a no-holds-barred declaration of war on the makers of Modern Art, using the sharpest weapon for the job: satire.

The poems in this booklet are varied, but then so is the hideousness of so much modern art. Some poems are executed with the precision of a boltgun, like Curtis' cod imitations. Others are blunter and leave you feeling like you've had a two-by-four applied to your frontal cortex, which is essentially the same feeling you get being introduced to the work of Walter Gropius or Robert Motherwell. Whatever device the subject calls for, Curtis applies it without holding back. The subject at hand demands nothing less.

Though this collection has an obvious offensive thrust against the agents of awful ideas, it is clear Curtis is most interested in defending something lovely—namely, art that uplifts, endures, and inspires, effects of art the modern variety rejects. In the spirit of deadly silliness, Curtis is among greats—Horace and Juvenal, Swift and Pope, Ogden Nash, and Dr. Seuss. None of the Modernist sacred cows, or balloons in the case of Jeff Koons, are safe. Nor should they ever have been.

MODERN ART: AN EXHIBITION IN CRITICISM

MODERN ART: AN EXHIBITION IN CRITICISM

SAVE ME, O LORD

Save me, O Lord, from the unyielding yoke
   Of kindness and care and profundity.
Save me from cautious and well-tempered jokes.
   O Lord, let me be funny.

Let me tell truth with the tip of a spear
   And quick jab without quarter or pity
The safe pretenses that hide in the ear.
   O Lord, let me be funny.

Let me strip naked the blue-stockinged prude,
   The middleclass Marxist conformity.
Let me trip Leninists, let me be rude.
   O Lord, let me be funny.

Please let me tickle the jabbering class
   And laugh at solemnous vanities.
Please let me quick poke peacockery's ass.
   O Lord, let me be funny.

Save me, O Lord, from the unditty ditty,
   From honestly felt pomposities.
Please save me from verses approved by committee.
   O Lord, let me be funny.

MODERN ART: AN EXHIBITION IN CRITICISM

PICTURE GALLERY

MODERN ART: AN EXHIBITION IN CRITICISM

CASIMIR MALEVICH
1866 – 1944

white paint on white

Malevich shows

black hole in sight

MODERN ART: AN EXHIBITION IN CRITICISM

PIET MONDRIAN
1872 – 1944

_____ He of lines and squares cubistic,
Mondrian, the neo-plastist' ....
_____ painted non-objective canvas
_____ rather something like Malevich ;
.... pictured canvases in So-Ho ....
pictured *Broadway Boogie Woogi e* ____ ,
.... and the critics wondered, "Would he
_____ win an everlasting glory ...... , __
.... be the new old new great master
__ .... __ now and then and ever-after .

_____ For he put the skin side outside ;
_____ hid the front-side-outside inside;
simplified all forms to four sides, ...
__ tinctured within four more straight lines .

____ Painter of the squareness sameness ,
painter of the colored flatness ....
ever never rounded color , ...
_____ painted squarer than all others ,
_____ painted red and white and yellow ,
painted green and black and yellow , ...
painted pictured patterns that show ....
_____ Mondrian's a simple fellow .

GERTRUDE STEIN
1872 – 1944

Pop-op Pollack. Please sneeze Napoleon,

lacks Napoleon, hacks Napoleon.

Pop up Pollack's knees la Napoleon

alla Pollock-Stein please, Napoleon.

Alla Pollock-Stein sneeze Napoleon.

MODERN ART: AN EXHIBITION IN CRITICISM

CONSTANTIN BRANCUSI
1876 – 1957

Few things are more snoozy than birds by Brancusi
except for his other whatsies and whosies,
the mish-mash of this and that stone and bright bronze
and other rough stuff that he would pile upon
the plates of the critics and the connoisseurs
who ate with delight this stuff from the sewers
and fed us the masses his smelly caprices
then bid we enjoy the great masterpieces
because they were polished for hours and hours,
because they are now worth millions of dollars,
and also because the critics are oozy —
but certainly not because they are choosy;
the musey-museums are all very fond
and were by the blathering easily conned:
Now as for myself, I'd rather we'd lose all the
whatsies and whosies and birds by Brancusi.

MIES VAN DER ROHE
1869 – 1960

The moderns love Miesy to piecies
for his numerous theories and theses:
   technological, clearly,
     yet boring and dreary.
A father of modern modernity,
   by buildings built boxy,
   black steely and glassy
made living unwholesome and ugly.

WALTER GROPIUS
1883 – 1960

What do you know about Gropius?

Why, he invented the Bauhaus:
   uncomfortable chairs,
   square without flair.

They function, but why all the fuss
o'er this graceless Gropius stuff?

   They are cold and faceless
   hard, empty spaces
that noy us in houses like Bah's house.

The sprawl of his malls are too copious
   and much too officious,
   too much prolifious,
and much, much presuppositious
   and Gropious.

FRANZ KLINE
1910 – 1962

O, please be kind.

Take my Frans Kline.

I won't mind.

WILLIAM CARLOS WILLIAMS
1883 – 1963

Who
depends too much
on the dew,
the wheel-barrow
Red, and you?

Which
chickens of white,
besides the itch
to write, glazed rain-
Water rich?

MODERN ART: AN EXHIBITION IN CRITICISM

TRISTAN TZARA
1896 – 1963

TzAra 's
tHe faDa
of DadA.

DAVID SMITH
1906 – 1965

O *Cubi II*,
who are you?

Are you the son
of *Cubi I*?

Or could you be
a *Cubi III*?

MODERN ART: AN EXHIBITION IN CRITICISM

LE CORBUSIER
1887 – 1965

Le Corbusier
was great, they say,
"The architect of his day."

He had ambition
and a mission;

he wrote editions,
won competitions,
designed with erudition;

made definitions,
had exhibitions
and expositions
of wacky compositions.

A rhetorician,
arithmetician
and geometrician;

a metaphysician
of juxtaposition.

The presupposition:
his houses, ya can't live in 'em.

MODERN ART: AN EXHIBITION IN CRITICISM

HANS HOFFMAN
1880 – 1966

hanshoff manfell offa cliffin_
                              1
                                   9
                                      6
                                          1

(*The Cliff*, oil on canvas, 1961)

ALBERTO GIACOMETTI
1901 – 1966

The footprint of the time-space man
    is a thing unending;
such is the universal plan
    of what had no beginning.

The statue is a form in space;
    thus, sculpture is the being.
As statues are to man to place,
    as object is to feeling.

That one exists cannot be proved,
    all knowledge is a theory;
The sense of non in platitude
    is vintage Giacometti.

MODERN ART: AN EXHIBITION IN CRITICISM

AD REINHARDT
1913 – 1967

Why write of Reinhardt?

"Reinhardt" rhymes with "art."

MARCEL DUCHAMP
1887 – 1968

Why Not Sneeze, Rose Salavay?

Duchamp Stripped Bare the Bride Today.

MARK ROTHKO
1903 – 1970

Rothko was a giant,
Rothko was a mint,
was hailed in print,
he made a dint,
I'll give a hint:
he's passé, don't buy int.

MODERN ART: AN EXHIBITION IN CRITICISM

BARNETT NEWMAN
1905 – 1970

Who's afraid of Barnett Newman's
Red and Yellow Stripes and Blue I.

PABLO PICASSO
1881 – 1973

Pee ca so so ca pee
O pee so ca so pee
so pee ca so pee O
pee so so ca so pee
ca so pee so pee so
O ca so pee ca so.

MODERN ART: AN EXHIBITION IN CRITICISM

ADOLPH GOTTLIEB
1903 – 1974

Mister master Adolph Gottlieb,
he the first with the disease,
Icantus Paintus So'ile Sneeze.

MODERN ART: AN EXHIBITION IN CRITICISM

ALEXANDER CALDER III
1898 – 1976

Calder's **mo bi les**
are not s t a **b** i l e **s**,
they are **f** ⁱ l **s**
    o   b   e .

MAN RAY
1890 – 1976

Man Ray made a bare lady play.

JOSEPH ALBERS
1888 – 1976

Joseph Albers squared a theory,
    boxed it in motif.
Framed a treatise daft and dreary,
    flat to read and see.
Black and beige and Bauhaus lifeless,
    yucked in Germany.
Praised to raise the green on priceless
    Mad Ave. in N.Y.C.

MODERN ART: AN EXHIBITION IN CRITICISM

JEAN ARP
1886 – 1976

Arp \ar-p\ n abbr Arp: 1: forms not sharp, but round 2: the artist found renown in forms made smooth 3: critics approved 4: not loud, in quiet formed to make no sounds; they make no sounds 5: now old they have holes not had when new; Arp <old> arping vb arpest arpt adj

MODERN ART: AN EXHIBITION IN CRITICISM

GIORGIO DE CHIRICO
1888 – 1978

De Chirico
by example shows:
although you can't paint
you still can be sold.

PEGGY GUGGENHEIM
1898 – 1979

A patroness extraordinaire,
the scion of a millionaire.
Peggy Guggenheim bought tidbits
for her walls to make exhibits
61st Street in New York.

And she collected modern artists,
handsome ones; brash, young, and strong.
New men: Arp, Cocteau, and Calder,
Marcel Duchamp, and Yves Tanguy,
Magritte, Kandinsky, and Max Ernst.

Some she loved, and some she married,
to some she paid a handsome fee;
to Baziottes, Motherwell,
Rothko, Pollock, and Clifford Still,
Gorky, Gottlieb, and Reinhardt too.

Of the many patronesses
who tasted the Moderne milieu,
none has had more cash successes
with Art of this past Century,
and none have housed more flesh than she.

MODERN ART: AN EXHIBITION IN CRITICISM

CLIFFORD STILL
1904 – 1980

Clifford Still did kill a painting.

When asked why, he said, "God made me."

MODERN ART: AN EXHIBITION IN CRITICISM

PHILIP GUSTON
1913 – 1980

Philip Guston must'a
neglected to clean his paint brushta.

MODERN ART: AN EXHIBITION IN CRITICISM

ANDY WARHOL
1928 – 1987

For we shall sing of Andy Warhol,
An artist mod, crass and commercial,
  A Campbell's shill,
  Albino ill,
Was Andy Warhol, whore to all.

HENRY MOORE
1898 – 1986

Holes are here and holes are there,
more holes than I've seen anywhere,

holed bellies of bronze, holed backs of wood,
Moore made 'em holes where e're he could:

So, Henry Moore made many holes,
though why he made 'em no one knows.

WILLIAM DE KOONING
1904 – 1988

William de Kooning
   might have been pleased
with a woman
   with multiple noses disease.
Yet as for myself,
'tis true, I prefer
   a she who grows pieces
   in all the right places
and puts all her parts
   just where they should be:
with a nose who knows
   it is not a knee,
   and by no means
   wears chattering teeth:
   whose beauty may be
imperfect but true,
   not goonie,
as William de Kooning once drew.

MODERN ART: AN EXHIBITION IN CRITICISM

SALVADOR DALI
1904 – 1989

Skid oup. The err with a Dali is that
it will eventually become a cat.

ROBERT MOTHERWELL
1915 – 1991

The paradox of Motherwell
   was the bigness of his painting:
     though mothered well were painted small,
though small were big in theory.

MODERN ART: AN EXHIBITION IN CRITICISM

FRANCIS BACON
1910 – 1992

Francis bakin'
made au gratin
from naughtin'.

Naught au bacon
Paintin' made a
Francis Bacon.

MODERN ART: AN EXHIBITION IN CRITICISM

JOHN CAGE
1912 – 1992

The song
  of John Cage:

a CaN aRy
  En CaGeD
nEvE r VaR iEs.

CLEMENT GREENBERG
1909 – 1994

Clement Greenberg says it's so.
Clement Greenberg did not know.
Clement Greenberg blowed and blowed
Thick as Clement Greenberg smoke:

*Pollock's strength lies in the emphatic
surfaces of his pictures, which it is his
concern to maintain and intensify in all
that fuliginous flatness which
began but only began — to be the strong
point of late cubism.*

Clement Greenberg let out air
Mod Art went *poof*. No one cares.
Clement Greenberg had his say.
Modern Art has passed away.

MODERN ART: AN EXHIBITION IN CRITICISM

RÖŸ LÏCHTËNSTËÏN
1923 – 1997

Röÿ Lïchtënstëïn pöppëd ä mïnd
ä-¨döttëd öf thë cömïc kïnd¨

MODERN ART: AN EXHIBITION IN CRITICISM

ROBERT RAUSCHENBERG
1925 – 2008

Observe
  ...a subliminal imitation of meaning
  transcending experience in imagination
  through the record of fact. And that, was quoting Rauschenberg.

ROBERT INDIANA
1928 – 2018

Robert Indiana of

the overdone land o' LOVE,
moved the middle **O** around

then copyrighted what he found.

BARBARA ROSE
1936 – 2020

No one knows
Modern pose
Barbara Rose.

MODERN ART: AN EXHIBITION IN CRITICISM

FRANK OWEN GEHRY
1929 –

```
O        g E h R y
         G e H r Y
         g E h R y
         G e H r Y  g
         G e H r Y
           e H r y
             r Y
         g E       Y
```

CLAES OLDENBERG
1929 –

Claes Oldenberg,
you will have heard,
ballooned
a plastic hamburger;
held its catsup,
held its lettuce,
served it sans
shake 'n French fries.
Hungry?
Well, with much regret
the thing will not be eaten;
if eaten, *yuck*,
it would be seen
as all such things
digested.

JASPER JOHNS
1930 –

Jasper Johns
paint and drew
his canvas on,
and cast a can
in painted bronze.

RICHARD SERRA
1938 –

A Modern Art slipped from the sky
upon a no-one passing by.

He should have moved, the artist said,
But he did not, so he is dead.

It seems we put Art in its place:
"Crush the public," the artists say.

MODERN ART: AN EXHIBITION IN CRITICISM

CINDY SHERMAN
1954 –

The cindy sherman made a name
by making of herself cliché.

MODERN ART: AN EXHIBITION IN CRITICISM

JEFFERY KOONS
1955 –

A Jeffery Koons
rhymes with "balloons".
And now you know
what is to know
of Jeffery Koons.

MODERN ART: AN EXHIBITION IN CRITICISM

CONCERT HALL

WHITMAN PROPOSES

Walt Whitman proposes
   poetic prose poses
A truth that transposes
   poetic prose poses:
To know what to know is
   to pose Whitman's poses.

Wit on Whitman
Sit on Whitman
Shhh... on Whitman

We know all the proses
   and all do now speak it
To pose is to posey
   unrhymed without wit:
We know modern poets
   in prosey do shhh...

Wit on Whitman
Sit on Whitman
Shhh... on Whitman.

Whitman was a poet
   everybody knows it
Like Whitman they will pose it
   to be a modern poet:
Propose: The pose is old bit
   and everybody knows it.

Wit on Whitman
Sit on Whitman
Shhh... on Whitman.

AVANT-GARDE MARCH

Ride on, Hegel. Ride on, Marx!
Ride on, ride on Alfred Barr.
Ride the magic Zeitgeist train
in this the avant-garde parade.

As the globe spins round and round
the avant-garde must not slow down;
we march till time and space collapse
then quickly, quickly we march backwards.

HEAR! HEAR! FOR THE SIN IN SINCERE

Hear! Hear! For the sin in sincere,
   For the lie in the truth,
   For the evil we do:
Hear! Hear! For the sin in sincere.

Hear! Hear! For the weakness and shame,
   For the spreading of blame
   Till we all sin the same:
Hear! Hear! For the weakness and shame.

Hear! Hear! For the freedom to sin,
   For the drugs and the sex,
   For the rap, rock and death:
Hear! Hear! For the freedom to sin.

Hear! Hear! For excuse and for blame,
   "No, it wasn't my fault
   For the anger I felt".
Hear! Hear! For excuse and for blame.

Hear! Hear! For the sin in sincere,
   I can honestly say
   That I screwed you today
Sincerely in sin my dears.
Hear! Hear! For the sin in sincere.

BARBARITY RENEWED

Denounce the old, proclaim the new,
Destroy the good, the bad debut,
   Logic torment,
   Let's all invent,
   Now hail the happy accident.

New music our sore torments,
It surely is not heaven sent:
   The banging drum,
   The Devil's hum
   From Hell it comes
To shake the world to dark descent,
The revolution to foment.

The vacant whale's echo tune,
Or pretended wisdoms of the loon.
   "Sing nature's song.
   You can't go wrong."
   Proclaims the back to Nature throngs.
Reject the capitalist goon.
Beneath the moon let's all commune.

Citizens of our New Age
Follow the new sage's rage:
Be free, have fun, melody shun,
And naked dance beneath the sun.

MODERN ART: AN EXHIBITION IN CRITICISM

Chisel's clink does not ring true,
Sculptors to object's error flew:
   Betray the soil,
   Never to toil.
   Smash, despise, despoil!
Volumes are old, objects are new,
So statues we bid you a tart, "Adieu!"

The painter's brush has run amuck,
It's stuffed with goop and filled with guck;
   Spattered with glee
   By chimpanzees
   Who own Picasso's pedigree.
The civilized to it say, "Yuck,
The painter's brush has run amuck."

Denounce the old, proclaim the new;
Destroy the good, the bad debut.
   Logic torment,
   Let's all invent,
   Now hail the happy accident.

The architect who once did build,
With beauty towns and cities filled,
   Uses computers,
   Invention neuters:
   Machines are the practitioners.
By repetition invention's stilled,
By ordinance is beauty killed.

Let's reinvent the sister-arts,
Break their bones, tear out their hearts,
   Sculpture upend,
   The buildings bend,
   And paintings rend,
On precedent let's turn our butts and fart!

So slap my back and let's shout, "Wee!"
Then raise a glass and toast to the
Great artists who new visions see –
The end of you, the end of me.

Sit silent in the theatre;
To Hollywood you must defer.
   Worship the stars.
   Seek the bizarre.
   Attend the Leftist seminar.
'Pon actors accolades confer,
You must concur. Death to the Dissenter!

From television we must learn
To accept, not to discern:
   Turn off the mind,
   Be the same kind
   As every other fool's behind.
Mindless let us all adjourn.
What you give to T.V., in return you earn.

Denounce the old, proclaim the new,
Destroy the good, the bad debut,
   Logic torment,
   Let's all invent,
   Now hail the happy accident.

Profess! To one-another sing.
On normal people scorn to fling
   With oozing ink
   The words which stink
   Of New Age think.
Upon the throat of virtue spring;
To be adverse is now the thing.

Or to repeat the latest phrase,
To be thought hip is all the craze:
   The one who cares,
   The one who shares,
   The one who the whole world repairs.
Professors blind lead through the maze,
They kiss the vague, they hug the haze.

Let's dance, let's sing, a New Age bring,
Let's all be loud, let's all be bores,
Mindless destroy what came before.
Let's tear it up, enjoy the gore.

No longer poet's voice aglow
With lightening flash, transcendent show;
   For truth they fear,
   Hold error dear,
   So no one hears:
They speak, but do not know.

To be lovely, to rhyme, they can't,
Stupid they blurt with awkward chant.
   Their voices drone
   In phrases groan,
   Grammar unknown.
A vision's lie, a doggish pant:
Poets today are silly things.

Denounce the old, proclaim the new,
Destroy the good, the bad debut,
   Logic torment,
   Let's all invent,
   Now hail the happy accident.

Now come and be tattooed:
Barbarity is renewed!

SAINT CECILIA JONES

One by one come beat the drum
Till millions, on millions, on millions come!
Boom. Boom! BOOM! We'll shake the room
And beat the drum till the walls fall in
And the ceiling comes down
And none of the pieces can be found!
So, Boom. Boom! BOOM! Come beat the drum!

We'll break the floors with angry feet,
Clap our hands, holler and scream,
Wiggle our tongues, let out a yell:
Ah-lay-lu, Ah-lay-lu, Ah-lay-lu-YA!
Across the mountains and over the plains
From sea to sea on Cecilia's Day!

So Sing to Saint Cecilia Jones,
Shinny your muscles and rustle your bones,
Chirp with the crickets, peep with the birds,
Hop on one foot with the buffalo herds,
Bounce on your butt, roll with the worms,
Kiss 'yer neighbor, exchange her germs!
Now everyone, both young and old,
Shake, rattle, and roll with Cecilia Jones!

MODERN ART: AN EXHIBITION IN CRITICISM

MULBERRY LANE

We walk to school on Mulberry Lane
No more, no more.
We skip and play with Spot, Dick, and Jane
No more, no more.
Put wheels on carts for Derby Days
No more, no more.
Don our bonnets for Easter Sundays
No more, no more.

The planet is dying,
The homeless are crying,
The taxes are rising,
The fruitcake is smiling,
The family is broken,
The home is broken,
And cities are broken,
Yet tech talk goes on, and on, and on, and on
While the drag queen is smiling
No more, no more.

The lawn is mowed and nobody knows
Where yesterday goes, when tomorrow will come.
The only hope is the day will be done
And the sun will shine when the weekend comes
No more, no more.

Shimmy-shimmy co-co-ba! Shimmy-shimmy ah!
Gimmie-gimmie co-co-ba! Gimmie-gimmie more!
Bounce with my sister,

Cover your blisters,
Mister kiss mister,
Cover your blisters
No more, no more.

Let us all wink at the cause of the week,
At the lines, at the lies, at the people who stink,
At the bribe, at the vote, at the smug, at the drunk,
But never, O never, dare take a walk
On Mulberry Street no more.

MODERN ART: AN EXHIBITION IN CRITICISM

LECTURE HALL

FOUR FREEDOMS OF MODERN ART

Freedom from Craft,
 from Responsibility,
Freedom from Intelligence
 and Ability.

CUBISM SQUARED

    ismcub
    sibcum
    muscib
    bicsum
    sicmub

cup let he to tub bed
pot bet heat cut lept
bed le bec tu up sept
the ta ble top cub ed

SO HO SO

So, So-Ho's
are silly.
Oh! So-Ho's.
See there those
old So-Ho's
are just so-so's.

FUTURISM FINISH

Futurism's
   the old
   retold
tired system

lipsticked new,
   yet cold
   like mold
and steel, too.

A BETTER JACKSON POLLOCK

The honors hung about the room
   In rows upon the walls;
The stylish modern shelves were strewn
   With testimonials
And other trinkets men will want,
But not the favor of a god.

Looking back from where he sat
   Over his long career
His eyes went blank as he leaned back
   Into his leather chair;
He took a gun from off his desk
And placed it up against his head.

Before he shot he had to move
   Some inches to the left
Lest the bullet should go through
   The picture he liked best;
Some copy of the last Saint John
A better man than he had done.

A click was heard but not the bullet
   That traveled through his brain
To strike some a la Mondrian
   He recently had made;
Which with blood and brains and splotches
Became a better Jackson Pollock.

THE COURSE UNFIRED

The moonlight streamed into the room
   And glowed on stars of dust,
All else was stuck as in a gloom,
   Her hands, the clay, a lump.
Her fingers still, they could not move
   Though thoughts spun round her mind.
Her will, unmoved; her flesh, a tomb;
   Her spirit, of the time.

"So why then cause to objects give?
   No cause to give is mine.
The void has set the purposes,
   Not mine to let them live.
Therefore, not me the tool of Spirit.
   Not I to understand.
My genius that I may forget
   Myself." And so she left.

The miracle of untouched lump
   Was spirited away.
A virgin pot, not got by fire.
   The critics were amazed;
Soon all the world did praise the un-
   Made testament in clay,
And this is why you see it here
   Exhibited today.

BEAT OF THE SCREAM

The beat of the scream of the song of the street
Rattles through flesh of whomever it meets.

The hum of machines like the bees on the green
Sting the ears and the mind in-between.

On the breeze hang aromas of filth and decay
From piles of bounty now rotting away.

Hot burns the sun on the cruel gray mead,
On the cage, on the cave, on the back of the beast

Whose temper erupts in a simian rage
To explode in rapping the street he made.

POETS SCRATCH

While I rest alone in quiet
   I hear the distant scratch
Of a hundred-thousand poets
   Writing trash.

And, although they went to college
   For training in their craft
Not one of them has known the god's
   Love or wrath.

Not a single spark has touched them
   Yet they scribble on and on,
Though none of us will miss them
   When they are gone.

MNEMOSYNE

"I don't believe in art. I believe in artists."
  Marcel Duchamp
  Art's Response: to M. Duchamp,
"Why sir should I believe in artists?"

STRIP THE POETS

No more glittering garments!
   Strip the poets
And let them stand bare naked
   Beneath spotlights.

Make them talk like us with
   Dust in their mouths,
Equality on their tongues
   Or shut them up.

PRAISE SONG

Busting the flute,
   breaking the glass,
rusting the metal
   wins the grant.
Wailing unpitched
   or speaking trash
and acting the fool
   wins the cash.
So steal if you like,
   poke in an eye:
Committing a crime
   gets the prize.
So burn the canvas,
   it's better that
the evidence
   does not last.
Praise the Endowment!
   the frauds and thieves
who steal from the poor
   to subsidize sleaze.

BUDDING MICHELANGELOS

Each enters bent and tilted halls,
rosed of cheek, of talent small,
upon a tinter's odyssey
because their parents paid the fee.
See budding Michelangelos
decked in spot bedappled clothes,
meandering like hatching lines
around the synapse of the mind
where the glory they imagine
yings and yangs with many changes,
changes like the op of color
from one thing into another:
into a check to pay the teachers
who dare not bruise the little creepers,
because the sots can fill the pot
with the stew their art could not.

POST ISM

Post
mod
ern
ism
ism
mod
ern
too.

MODERN ART: AN EXHIBITION IN CRITICISM

XXTH CENTURY MODERN SPEAKS

Gnarled, tired, witless and old, the graybeard questions:
Is civilization a vain and futile occupation?

O! once when I was young I fashioned dreams,
exquisite machines, and complex philosophies.

When grown, I in anger spat, burned the past,
built a world in my own damn image, new and fast.

I was modern, hard as steel, quick as lightening.
Now at the close, I stall confused, old arguments tightening

while a frightening prospect stands before me and I
totter on the edge of the piss abyss, soon to collapse.

Damn—damn you. Damn! The New shall not come again.
I will not be old. When I die all will end

forever, damn you.

SPOKEN AT THE DEDICATION: ART MUSEUM ADDITIONS, 1940-2005

Tilt the boxes,
Bend the wall,
Bust the columns,
Crush them all;
Break tradition,
Hide the art;
Our museums
Come apart.
Ain't we clever,
Ain't we smart.

MODERN ART: AN EXHIBITION IN CRITICISM

SLOW THE WIT

Slow the wit of dirtied brushes
When wielded by untutored splotchers;
Dull the ding of hammered metals
Unshaped by tin-eyed pre-submentals.
Hear, like winded leaves the dollars
Fall sick from rotted wallet bowers:
Asphalt, you know, is nature barren —
Hidden *isms* are here unriddled.

Splotch'd paint upon the pants
Are oh so many seething ants
Word-like unstitched upon the air
Dissolve as if t'were never there.
So many leaflets, so much ink
Swirl like spirals in open sinks
Through dizzy ears into the veins
And through the bowels to splotch again.
Splotch on splotch the splotches grow,
Stink awhile, are praised then go
Into a classroom where they hide:
A carcass rots, unsprings a mind,
Tickless the ghost dissolves in time.
Unfleshed in heaps lie well picked bones,
The gawkers stare and then drive on,
For no one cares the Times are done.

The coffin's top — the rotten door,
Kicked, not fallen to the floor.
The ground a graveyard of the mind,

A granite dull and dark inside.
Outside is carved the epitaph,
"You came, you saw, you laughed, you left."
A rusty nail is hammered in
The coffin's top; *tap, tap*; the end.

   Who is left to praise or blame,
Which witless thought, which puffed-up name —
All silly braggarts who drop their drawers
To dance their sausage about the floor,
You know, the stage, the play of fools —
See them costumed, hear them boom
And bellow all the braggart hordes
Once too much, and we are bored.

SO LONG WORDS: MODERN ART MONOGRAPHS

Words of words and words in words
    Wording nowhere, meaning "nothing".
Written, spoken and no word heard;
No one listened to wording words
    Unworthy of a second printing.

Books of books and books assigned
    Picturing big printed pictures,
Pics like twisted turned intestines
That will not rhyme or scan on time
    Alike an angel's pin-headed lecture.

And on and on and on they drone,
    In Art Modern music and pics,
The pat pretentious phrases coined
Then unremembered in non in sense
    Which, if not for laughs would make you sick.

Word many words, book many books,
    Pic many pics then drone you on
At those the few who peep a look
In shows, in class, in halls at books
    To drone alone: Mod echo on.

THE NEW MOO: STOCK MODERNISM

Come children, hear the moo,
the art of the post-new,
the weird advanced milieu
that grew from the Mod zoo.
"Moo New," the critics moo,
"Moo art is the Post-New."

RAISON D'ÊTRE

Iconoclasts exist
as long as icons last.

The idols all are broke
so Modern Art's a joke.

With nothing more to brake
d'être has gone away.

With all of raison said
the Modern Art is dead.

AVANT-GARDE LAMENT

We thought the train was speeding
  when we hurried *click-clack* by
for we were the advance guard
  yahoos could not pass by
because we nailed the theory
  because we laid the tracks
yes! we were the advanced guard
  so how can we be passed.

MODERN FACE

The glass-crete is the modern face
   Whose steel eyes are ice.
The structures of the modern place
   Are stark and hard, not nice.

Once moderns built in boxes
   Too straight till some were crook'd.
Today the modern box is
   A toddler's project ripped.

Some smold yet like an outhouse
   Flattened out and vacant,
Folded up and iron loused,
   And Gehry's are abhorrent:

Bent socked bulbous museums,
   His bumbling additions,
Dull wits of those who see 'em –
   Like patrons of the Corcoran,
Our cities once were honor seen,
   Inspiring and ennobled,
Like visions some great God had dreamed.
   Our cities now are dumbled,
   Like Gehry bent and fumbled.

MUST WE

Must we have a serious tone?
Must we have a serious drone?
Must we every-time unrhyme?
   Unmeter our feet to undo
   All that was done to be new?
All that was done, all that was said
Lies within us; never is dead.
As long as I live may this be true:
He did all things well, nothing new.

EXTRACTED EX PRESSIONS

Ex	press	ions		
ab	stract	ed		
ex	tract	ed		
axp	ress	ions,		
an'	that	did.		

Ex	ab	ex	axp	an'
press	stract	tract	ress	that
ions	ed	ed	ions,	did.

MINIMALIST

He never lived,
he never died,
he never cried,
he never rhymed,
he never did,
he never didn't,
he never would,
because he couldn't.

CENSOR ME

"Censor me, O censor me!"
   the modern artists cry.
"If you would but censor me,
   my middling work
   the public would buy.
O, how I loathe the bourgeoisie:
Censor! O please censor me."

RING OUT THE NEW 1900

Another hundred years has gone
With all the other ones
Into the annals of the past
To rest at last.

The happy promise of the new
We rang in with much ado,
And yet the newness did not dawn:
Analysts were wrong.

So, wiser now we bid adieu
To the old-modern new:
For modern did as modern does,
Now the modern was.

MODERN ART: AN EXHIBITION IN CRITICISM

ABOUT THE AUTHOR

A sculptor, painter, historian, architectural designer, and poet, Michael Curtis has taught and lectured at universities, colleges, and museums, including The Institute of Classical Architecture & Art, The Center for Creative Studies, and The National Gallery of Art. His pictures and statues are housed in over 400 private and public collections, including The Library of Congress, The National Portrait Gallery, and The U.S. Supreme Court. He has made statues of presidents, generals, Supreme Court justices, captains of industry and national heroes, including Davey Crockett, General Dwight D. Eisenhower, and Justice Thurgood Marshall. His reliefs and medals include depictions of Presidents Harry S. Truman and Ronald Reagan, Justice John Marshall, and George Washington. Curtis' *History of Texas*, containing over one-hundred figures, is the largest American relief sculpture of the 20th century.

His monuments and memorials, buildings, and houses (including The New American Home, 2011), are found coast-to-coast. His plays, essays, verse and translations have been published in over 30 journals (*Trinacria*, *Society of Classical Poets*, *Expansive Poetry*, and others), and his most recent nonfiction books are *Occasional Poetry: How to Write Poems for Any Occasion* (available from The Studio Press) and *The Classical Architecture and Monuments of Washington, D.C.* (available from The History Press). Websites where Curtis' work can be found include The Classical Artist (theclassicalartist.com—art, architecture, and design), The Studio Press (thestudiobooks.com—essays and books in fiction and exposition, verse, and prose), and The Beautiful Home (the-beautiful-home.com—history, lifestyle, architecture, and design).

Curtis is the National Civic Art Society's 2021-2022 Research Fellow.

Made in the USA
Middletown, DE
30 March 2022